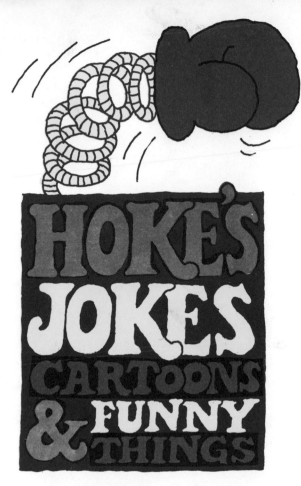

HOKE'S JOKES CARTOONS & FUNNY THINGS

by
HELEN HOKE

Pictures by
ERIC HILL

FRANKLIN WATTS | NEW YORK | LONDON

Library of Congress Cataloging in Publication Data

Hoke, Helen, 1903—
    Hoke's jokes, cartoons & funny things.

    SUMMARY: Poems, cartoons, riddles, puns, and tongue twisters which include "Fifty-four fat friars fanning furious flames."
    1. Wit and humor, Juvenile. [1. Wit and humor. 2. Joke books] I. Hill, Eric, illus. II. Title.
PZ8.7.H63Ho3   [817]   74-7459
ISBN 0-531-02682-5

Grateful thanks are due to the following for permission to reproduce cartoons: Associated Newspapers; The *Sunday Mirror*; *Boy's Life*; *Saturday Evening Post*; *News of the World*; Syndication International; *Daily Mirror*; London Express News and Features.

First published in London by Franklin Watts, Ltd. 1973.
First American publication by Franklin Watts, Inc., 1975.

HOKE'S JOKES CARTOONS & FUNNY THINGS

Dumb: Will you join me in a bowl of soup?

Dumber: Do you think there'd be room in there for both of us?

Sally: Why do you run around with your stockings full of holes like that?

Molly: I don't give a darn.

There was an old man from Peru,
Who dreamt he was eating his shoe.
He awoke in the night
In a terrible fright,
And found it was perfectly true!

Long ago there was a cat,
Who swallowed a ball of yarn,
And when the cat had kittens,
They all had sweaters on.

Little Paul, bragging: My mother is very smart—
she can sew and knit and crochet—and tattoo.

*   *   *

Silly: What ball can't
you play with?
Billy: An eye ball.

TONGUE-TEASERS
(Say these three times — FAST!)

Peter's plump Persian plum
fizzed past fast.

Soldiers shoveling soft snow slowly.

Fifty-four fat friars fanning furious flames.

Lily lisps listlessly and lazily.

Bisquick, kiss quick! quick kiss.

* * *

Little Boy to visitor: It must be rather difficult
to eat soup with such a big moustache.
Visitor: Yes. It's quite a strain.

Curious Benny: What holds the moon up?
Smart Denny: The moon-beams, of course.

Frank: Have you ever met my sister, Molly?
Hank: Yes. She's the fat one, isn't she?
Frank: Yes—but I have another sister, Lena.

THE FIDDLING CAT

A cat came fiddling
    Out of a barn,
With a pair of bagpipes
    Under her arm;
She could sing nothing
    But "fiddle-cum-fee,
The mouse has married
    The bumblebee;"
Pipe, cat; dance, mouse!
We'll have a wedding
    At our good house.

Romantic Rena: What two beaux can *every* girl have?
Sour Sal: El-bows.

*   *   *

Jerry: Did you ever see the
        Catskill Mountains?
Terry: No, but I've seen them kill mice.

"Who is it?"

MOCK MEANINGS

Caterpillar: A worm wearing a sweater.

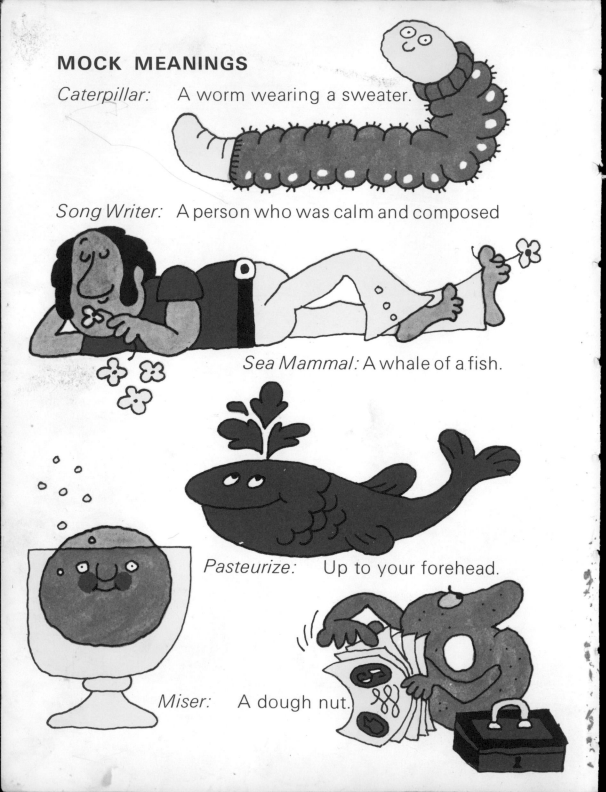

Song Writer: A person who was calm and composed

Sea Mammal: A whale of a fish.

Pasteurize: Up to your forehead.

Miser: A dough nut.

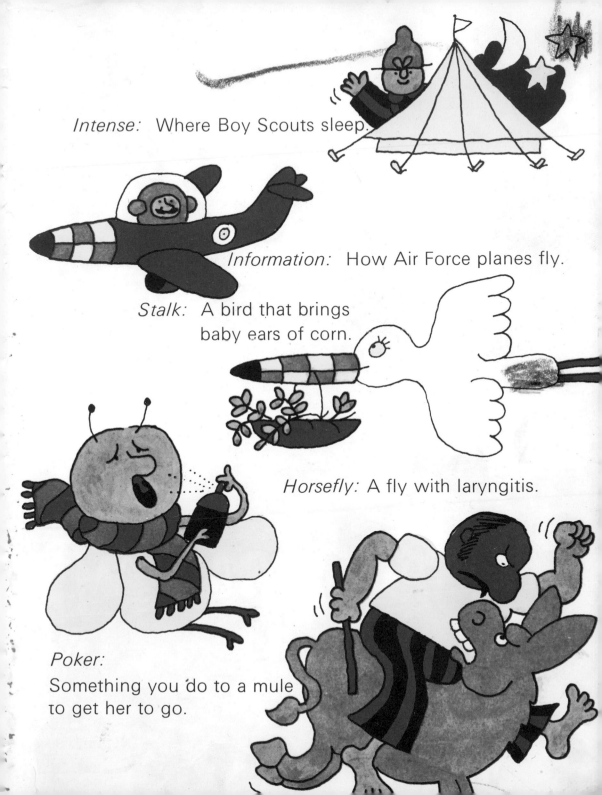

Intense: Where Boy Scouts sleep.

Information: How Air Force planes fly.

Stalk: A bird that brings baby ears of corn.

Horsefly: A fly with laryngitis.

Poker: Something you do to a mule to get her to go.

Weary mother to a group of
wild children at a birthday party:
   "There is a special prize for the
one who goes home first!"

Arty: Did you hear about the fight on
the train?
Smarty: Yes. The inspector punched
a ticket.

Elvis:
When is an operation funny?
Pelvis:
When it leaves the patient in stitches.

Curious Carl: What is a volcano?
Smart Sue: Easy . . . a mountain with hiccups.

"Next time I come around for the rent I want money"

YUMMY!
I love my wife and I love my baby,
I love my biscuits sopped in gravy.

What did one elevator say to the other?
"I think I'm coming down with something."

Why did the lady sew labels saying "cotton"
in all her wool suits and coats?
She wanted to fool the moths.

"After the ambulance left, we all had a good laugh when kitty climbed from the tree by itself."

ACKEN.

WHEN DARE YOU SNEEZE?

Sneeze on Monday, sneeze for danger;
Sneeze on Tuesday, kiss a stranger;
Sneeze on Wednesday, get a letter;
Sneeze on Thursday, something better;
Sneeze on.Friday, sneeze for sorrow;
Sneeze on Saturday, see your sweetheart tomorrow.
SNEEZE ON SUNDAY, YOU'LL HAVE COMPANY!

WHOSE DOG? WHOSE CAT?

There was a man, and his name was Dob,
And he had a wife, and her name was Mob,
And he had a dog, and he called it Cob
And she had a cat called Chitterabob.
Cob, says Dob.
Chitterabob, says Mob.
Cob was Dob's dog,
Chitterabob Mob's cat.

Anonymous

Boastful Bob, telling a story: On my right hand was a lion, on my left was a tiger, in front and at the back of me were wild elephants.

Gullible Gus: What happened?

Boastful Bob: Then the merry-go-round stopped.

Dummy: If a butcher was seven feet tall and wore size thirteen shoes, what would he weigh?

Brighty: Meat, stupid.

BE CAREFUL!

If you should meet a Crocodile
   Don't take a stick and poke him,
Ignore the welcome in his smile,
   Be careful not to stroke him.
For as he sleeps upon the Nile,
   He thinner gets and thinner,
And whene'er you meet a Crocodile
   He's ready for his dinner.

Anonymous

"Yours melted on the way back"

Georgie: What is a mosquito with the itch?
Porgie: A jitterbug.

Smart: What has keys and can't open locks?
Smarter: Monkeys, turkeys, and donkeys.

MR. FINNEY'S TURNIP

Mr. Finney had a turnip
    And it grew behind the barn;
And it grew and it grew,
    And that turnip did no harm.

There it grew and it grew
    Till it could grow no longer;
Then his daughter Lizzie picked it
    And put it in the cellar.

There it lay and lay
    Till it began to rot;
And his daughter Susie took it
    And put it in the pot.

And they boiled it and boiled it
As long as they were able;
And then his daughters took it
And put it on the table.

Mr. Finney and his wife
They sat them down to sup;
And they ate and they ate
And they ate that turnip up!

Anonymous

TWEEDLE-DUM AND TWEEDLE-DEE

Tweedle-dum and Tweedle-dee
 Resolved to have a battle,
For Tweedle-dum said Tweedle-dee
 Had spoiled his nice new rattle.
Just then flew by a monstrous crow,
 As big as a tar-barrel,
Which frightened both the heroes so
 They quite forgot their quarrel.

Lewis Carroll

Educated Eddie: When did Caesar reign?
Dumb Dora: I didn't know he rained.
Educated Eddie: Of course! Didn't they hail him!

City Visitor: Why do you go over the potatoes with such a heavy roller?
Farmer: Because I want to grow mashed potatoes this year.

Izzy: Why is it a mistake to gossip in a stable?

Dizzy: Because all horses carry tails.

"You might have explained it was a stuck mouth organ I was to pull out before letting me fill 57 cavities".

Mrs. New-Rich, at a bridge tea-party: I clean my diamonds with ammonia, my rubies with wine, my emeralds with brandy, and my sapphires with fresh cream.

Mrs. Long-Rich, quietly: I don't clean my jewelry at all. When mine gets dirty I just have my butler throw it away.

Fond Uncle: How old are you, little Bobby?

Bobby: Four-and-a-half.

Fond Uncle: My, my! Nearly five years old—and you're no taller than my umbrella.

Bobby: How old is your umbrella?

Nell: What vegetable needs a plumber?

Mell: Easy—a leek.

Andy: When is a black dog not a black dog?
Sandy: When he's a grey-hound.

Worried Willy: How did Little Bo-Peep lose her sheep?
Silly Sue: She had a crook with her.

Teacher: We know that the ruler of Russia was called the Czar and his wife the Czarina. Now, what were their children called?

Pupil: Czardines.

*   *   *

I asked my mother for fifty cents
To see the elephant jump the fence.
He jumped so high he reached the sky,
And didn't get back till the Fourth of July.

"There's probably quite a commotion at home by now. I locked myself in the bathroom and climbed out of the window."

Expensive Wife, ordering a new hat: What kind of bird shall I have on it?
Worried Husband: One with a small bill.

On which side does a chicken have the most feathers?

The outside.

WRAP YOUR TONGUE AROUND THESE:

Jim, the thin twin tinsmith.

The black bank-book blew back.

Timothy thrust sheaves into the threshing machine.

Rarely does roly-poly Rowley run his road-roller.

A big mixed-biscuit box.

Shingles and singles: shave a single shingle thin.

      ★   ★   ★

Molly: Why is a good cabbage generous?
Polly: Because it has a big heart.

"There! What's so hard about clearing a table?"

Jokey Jenny: When does a chair dislike you most?
Jolly Joe: When it cannot bear you.

★   ★   ★

Eager Eddie: Would you rather an elephant attacked you or a gorilla?

Nervous Neddie: I'd rather the elephant attacked the gorilla!

Curious Ken: How does the fireplace feel
when you fill it with coal?
Clever Chris: Grate-full, naturally.

Sleepy Pam: How can you keep a rooster
from crowing on Monday morning?
Smart Sam: Easy—eat him for Sunday dinner.

"I think we'll have to re-set it"

Country Boy: I like to go to bed and get up with the chickens, don't you?

City Boy: No, I like to sleep in my own bed.

Waitress: Are you very Hungary?

Traveler: Yes, Siam.

Waitress: Well, we'll be glad to Fiji. What can I Serbia?

Traveler: I'll have some Chile and Aix and coffee. And be sure to Sweden the coffee with a Cuba sugar.

Silly: Here's a telegram from the boss in Africa. He says he is sending us some lions' tails.

Willy: Lions' tails? What are you talking about?

Silly: Well, read it yourself. It says, "Just captured two lions. Sending details by mail."

"I think you've misunderstood the role you play in this."

Visitor, in drug store: I'll take a cake of soap.
Salesman: Scented or unscented?
Visitor: I'll take it with me.

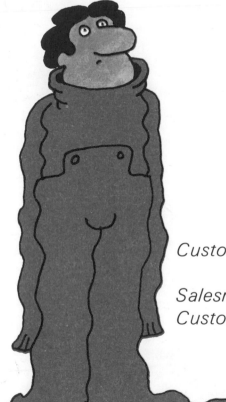

Customer: I want some long winter underwear.
Salesman: How long, sir?
Customer: How *long*? I don't want to *rent* 'em—I want to *buy* 'em.

Little Brother: Are you a suitor for my sister's hand?
Sister's Beau: Yes, but I didn't.
Little Brother: Didn't what?
Sister's Beau: Suit her.

Smart: I don't like this cold weather.
Smarter: Oh, it's nothing.
Smart: What are you talking about? . . . It's zero.
Smarter: Well, *that's* nothing.

Young Man: You look sweet enough to eat.
Pretty Girl: I *do* eat. Where'll we go?

Sandy: Name me three kinds of nuts.
Andy: That's easy! Peanuts, walnuts—
and forget-me-nuts.

*   *   *

Rosie: What grows up while it grows down?
Josie: A baby duckling.

Scared Sidney:

I lost Mama's bracelet and she'll be awful mad if shiver finds out.

"We'd prefer something on the floor above . . ."

"I wish it would bury its bones like other dogs!"

Dopey, at the theatre: Now, what is your best trick?

Magician: I saw a woman in half.

Dopey: Is it difficult?

Magician: It's child's play. I learned it as a child.

Dopey: Are there any more children at your home?

Magician: I have several half-sisters.

*   *   *

Teacher: What makes petrified trees?
Pupil: Perhaps high winds make them rock.

Quizzical Carl: I bet you don't know
what goes around
a button.
Educated Eddie: Pooh! Easy—a goat,
goes around
a-buttin', of course.

Doleful Dan: This match won't light.
Curious Carl: What's the matter with it?
Doleful Dan: I don't know, it worked a minute ago.

Clever Carl:
Why did the farmer call his rooster "Robinson?"
Clever Clara:
Easy . . . because he crew so.

What is the most striking thing in the way of a mantel ornament?
A clock.

Angry Landlady: I think you had better board elsewhere.

Boarder: Yes, I often have.

Angry Landlady: Often had *what?*

Boarder: Had better board elsewhere.

Dopey Diana thinks the four seasons are pepper, salt, oil and vinegar.

Mother: Sonny, I can't hear you saying your prayers.
Sonny: Well, I wasn't talking to you.

* * *

Jokey Joe: What did one eye say to the other?
Jolly Jane: Just between you and me, there's
something that smells.

Over a British telephone:
    "Are you there?"
    "Who are you, please?"
    "Watt."
    "What's your name?"
    "Watt's my name."
    "Yes, what's your name?"
    "My name is John Watt."
    "John what?"
    "Yes."
    "I'll be around to see you this afternoon."
    "All right. Are you Jones?"
    "No, I'm Knott."
    "Will you tell me your name then?"
    "Will Knott."
    "Why not?"
    "My name is Knott."
    "Not *what*?"

"Yes, he went back to school today—and I'm not sorry the holidays are over"

Teacher: What is an octopus?
Young Billy, after thinking it over quite a while:
An eight-sided cat.

"You can't possibly miss it—it's the only burning house in the road"

Billy: How did you meet your girl?

Silly: Oh, we got caught in a revolving door and started going around together.

*　　*　　*